BOSS MOMS
MOVE
DIFFERENTLY

**REDEFINE MOTHERHOOD.
REPRIORITIZE YOUR WELL-BEING.
REINVENT YOUR LIFE.**

Robyn Jones Woods, MBA, SHRM-SCP

ISBN: 979-8-218-14051-9

Boss Mom Moves Workbook

In addition to the book, I've created a Boss Mom Moves Workbook that will help you implement the strategies covered throughout the book. Visit www.bmmdbook.com/resources to download your copy today.

Dedication

I dedicate this book to my dad Roosevelt Jones, my mom Edna Jones, and my brother Russell Jones. You inspire me to live my truth unapologetically and reach my fullest potential while on earth. I will forever be grateful for the love, support, and times that we shared as a family. As I live out my truth, I hope that my example will encourage other women to do the same.

To my loving and incredible husband, Antoine Woods, I thank you for your support and your commitment to our family and me. I thank you for speaking life into me and for being my rock during some of the most challenging moments in my life. I'm truly grateful that God brought us together.

To my beautiful children, Aubrie and Evan, I am pledging to be the fullest version of myself so I can give you my best. I hope you never settle for the status quo. I believe you have the potential to achieve greatness and make a difference in this world. I want you to know that even if Mama doesn't have all the answers, one thing you can be sure of is that I will always be committed to self-development and becoming the best version of myself so I can serve our family. I love you forever and always.

To my brothers, Steven Jones and Randy Jones, I'm thankful for your support in my personal and professional endeavors. Thank you for not giving up on life when our faith was tested. I'm thankful that we decided to move forward and not allow the tragedies of life to stop us. Daddy, Mama, and Rujo would be so proud of us. I look forward to seeing what else God has in store.

To my mother-in-law, Elaina Woods, who has always treated me as if I were her own, my amazing family, friends, and church family, thank you all for your prayers and continued support. To my business besties, who are committed to being their best, flourishing, and never settling when it gets uncomfortable - You women have paved the way for so many of us and that means more than you know. You inspire me to do the same.

Table of Contents

Introduction

I'm a Boss Mom. You may have heard that phrase before, but I'll tell you right now it's not just a title. It's a mindset, a self-care journey, and a way to live life differently than the average mom.

As a Boss Mom, you are a leader and a high achiever, and you desire to be the best version of yourself. You take risks and believe in personal growth. It's time for you to fully become the boss of your life. Bosses who move differently don't settle for mediocrity. We're ambitious, confident, make tough decisions, and know what it takes to live the life we want.

Research suggests that the quality of the relationship between a mother and child can significantly impact children's outcomes. Children who have a close and supportive relationship with their mothers tend to have better outcomes in terms of their emotional well-being. Mothers who provide a secure and supportive environment for their children can help them feel safe and loved and foster their self-esteem and confidence. When we aren't emotionally available to our children due to the demands of our day, it takes a toll on our children's well-being over time. My goal in this book is to help women find more moments to connect with themselves and their children so that they can establish stronger families and communities. Our children need the reassurance that we are available to help them navigate the complexities of life, or else they'll eventually find other avenues to be seen, heard, and understood.

You may find it challenging to do what you love or be present in your home for your children, spouse, significant other, or even family members and friends. You find yourself barely getting by on the weekends, and you hardly have any time to enjoy yourself. You may be looking for more fulfillment in your work, but you're too afraid to pivot because of the financial risks involved. You often find yourself being everything to everybody. Some of your dreams may have been put on the back burner because you may be experiencing a setback due to job loss, illness, or death. I can relate to most of these because, over the past 10 years, I've had to overcome many adversities.

The turning point for me was when my mother, father, and brother's life was taken unexpectedly. As anyone could imagine, it was a traumatizing moment for me and my family. I was devastated and left with many questions about life, religion, and family. Because I was expecting to get married four days after this tragedy, I began to question my existence (the way I would show up) as a future wife and mother. Should I depend on my spouse to take care of me as my father did for us? Am I capable of becoming the meek, spiritual, and praying woman that my mother was? Am I mentally capable of raising a family? If my mother sacrificed most of her life for the sake of her family, was that all I had to look forward to in motherhood? Thinking this way put me in moments of depression because, for the longest time, I couldn't see past my current situation of depression and confusion after experiencing the loss of my family. I wondered who I would become as a mother and if I could eventually heal from the loss of my family.

I also had questions as a career woman. Should I pursue this exciting business endeavor that can pay far more than what I can imagine, or do I stay in this unfulfilling career that barely pays the bills? Should I put these bachelor's and master's degrees to work and pursue this career until my children graduate high school, or should I take a chance on myself and start the business I've wanted to pursue for years?

In this moment of transition between losing my loved ones and starting a new life of marriage, I felt compelled to answer questions that I had never thought about previously. I felt like I needed to choose, but the answers didn't seem to come easily. After I finally decided to start a family, I found myself unable to answer most of the questions playing out in my mind. It took hours of therapy, several setbacks, disappointments, and sick days before I began to approach my life differently.

The Best Cake Ever

Anyone who knows me knows how much I love a good cream cheese pound cake. I have been using a family recipe for years. It was passed down from my grandmother, who passed it to my mother and her sisters. In my early twenties, a cream cheese pound cake was something that I often baked with my mother. As I became a mom, I didn't have as many opportunities to bake with my children as toddlers, but now that they are school-aged, I use holidays for baking cakes with them.

Around Christmas 2022, I baked a cake and hadn't done so in about a year. When it was finished, I couldn't understand why the cake didn't come out as expected. I called my grandmother and aunts who verified that I had used the right ingredients. After speaking with my grandmother, I concluded that the cake wasn't coming out right because I had an oven or cake pan issue.

In December, my family came together to celebrate my grandmother's 90th birthday. As we were finishing dinner, I finally built up the courage to ask a few family members about the cream cheese pound cake recipe. It bothered me that I couldn't get it right. And because my uncle who makes the best cakes was present, I figure he'd chime in to share his thoughts. My grandma, aunt, and I were all going through the recipe together. I confirmed with them that the ingredients were correct. For a split second, I thought maybe there was a secret ingredient no one was telling me about.

Finally, my uncle intervened and told me that I was not mixing the ingredients in the right order. He explained how to mix the cake using a process that left most of us with perplexed looks on our faces. I could tell that my grandmother wanted to interject, but she didn't. My uncle looked at us and said, "I know it may seem unorthodox because this is how you've always been taught to make the cake. But if you want the best cake, you've got to mix it differently."

If you are into baking cakes, you probably know from looking at different recipes on Google (or cookbooks) that there are multiple ways to mix a cake. I had no idea! Cakes can be baked in various ways, each technique resulting in a different final product. After the conversation with my uncle, I was determined to try out his method as soon as I could.

The next day, my children and I anxiously prepared the ingredients for the cake and got to work. The process shared by my uncle took much longer than what I had been accustomed to. As I continued to add ingredients in the order my uncle suggested, the consistency of the cake began to change into a texture I wasn't familiar with. It was at this point that I began to doubt everything he had shared the previous night. My children had even gotten discouraged and were ready to throw in the towel because the mixture didn't look right.

I attempted to call my uncle and a few aunts who were present during the cake discussion, but no one answered. I finally took a breath and reminded my children that my uncle had warned us that the mixture wouldn't look like what we were used to, but to trust the process. As bad as I wanted to give up on the cake, the thought of the current egg prices gave me the ammunition I needed to keep going.

About 20 minutes into the process, the texture began to appear smooth as I remembered. After pushing through a two-hour process of mixing and baking the cake, it was finally ready to take out of the oven. The first taste of this cake melted in your mouth, just like my uncle's did. It was one of the best cakes I'd ever made. Although the process created moments of uncertainty, my family and I were happy that we pushed through.

Why am I sharing this story? In life, we are handed a recipe. To get the delicious, perfectly baked cake you desire, you must ensure that you have the right ingredients. If the cake's ingredients aren't exactly right, your cake may not turn out as you expected. Sometimes it may take using the ingredients differently and not following the original recipe you were handed. Think about it this way. The recipe for a cake represents the scripts that have been written in your mind based on influences and experiences in your life. The ingredients symbolize the thoughts, actions, decisions, and resources used to create a specific outcome in your life.

It all boils down to this one thing. You can make all the difference in your life by examining what you bring to it. If you're not satisfied with the outcomes in your life, change your recipe! Every person has a recipe for success. Some people use the same ingredients but produce different outcomes because they choose to use the ingredients in a different way. You may have recipe elements that don't work or want to experiment with a new recipe altogether. Either way, it's important to think about how you use each ingredient so you can achieve your best outcome.

Sis, you are more than a mom. You are more than a wife, and you don't have to play small. This is your opportunity to tap into your greatness and elevate beyond your current situation. You are a highly driven woman and you've grown in your career or business, but you still have doubts about how far you can go because you've started a family. It's ultimately our responsibility to model healthy motherhood and prioritize our well-being so our children can grow up to be better versions of us. If you have daughters, think about what you want to model for them as future moms.

By the end of this book, I hope you will have established the meaning of motherhood and success in your life. You don't have to accept the limitations placed on you as a woman and a mother. You can do the things you love, have the things you desire, and become your best self now while raising a family. You don't have to suffer in silence or function on autopilot.

If you read this book and implement the strategies shared, my prayer is that it will change the mindsets that have been holding you back from finding fulfillment in your day-to-day life. You will speak, think, plan, decide, grow, and move differently. You will become the boss of your life.

Chapter 1

The Mama Myths

*"The perfect mother doesn't exist, but there are
a number of ways to be a great one."*

- Robyn Woods

Mama Myths

I grew up in a household with my mother and father, who devoted most of their time to our family, the church, and their teaching careers. I was the only girl out of five children. My mother was my first motherhood influence and represented what many would call the "Proverbs 31" woman. She was a virtuous woman of character. She was the rock of our family. She was the type of woman who would get up before the crack of dawn to pray and meditate on God's word and be the last to go to bed at night. My Mother was the epitome of a Boss Mom. I am still in awe of how she mastered raising five children, keeping the house together, working full-time as an elementary school teacher, assisting with homework, volunteering at church/community events, and attending our extracurricular activities. Now don't get me wrong, my father was also very present in our home. I saw both of my parents partnering to raise our family. I didn't realize how blessed I was to have witnessed such a partnership between a husband and wife as a child.

In my church community, most of the mothers were working moms like my mother. As I became a teenager, I began to notice how my friends spent time with their mothers. Some of my friends spent time on the weekends with their mothers getting their nails done, or shopping. My friends whose mothers worked on the weekends barely got to spend time with them. Others, like me, had mothers who could barely carve out time to do anything outside of going to church, taking their children to the hairdresser/barber shop, or shopping for groceries.

Me and my mother's relationship grew apart as I became older. We didn't have many intimate talks or conversations because I was in my teenage world, and my mother was busy wearing many hats of the family. Looking back, I realize it was almost impossible for her to be emotionally available because she had nothing left to give.

Out of all the things I saw my mom doing for our family and everyone else, I barely saw her taking time out for herself. I can recall buying gift cards for her to get mani/pedis, but she never used them. I would try to convince her to go with me to the salon as we got older, but she wouldn't go. I can vividly remember arguments between my mother and I about her not going out to do things for herself. She never said it, but it was almost as if my mother didn't feel deserving of having time for herself.

I didn't start seeing my parents travel, go on dates, or tap into social circles until all of us were out of the house. I share this because many of the things I witnessed with how my mom raised our family and took care of herself influenced how I showed up as a mother during the early years of my motherhood journey. I can't put into words how much I love and miss my mother. She was my biggest supporter, taught me how to lead with love and respect, and showed me that what you do (not what you say) matters most. Because of this, she continues to be a massive inspiration in my life.

She made such an impact on many other women in our community, but after losing her, my dad, and my brother, I couldn't help but think about how my mom's life would have been if she had taken more time for herself. When we were younger, she often seemed tired and stressed out.

How would life have been different if she hadn't waited until she was well into her sixties to start traveling or starting her new hobby of crocheting? How would she have spent her life if she had leaned on her friends and community more to help her with us so that she wouldn't be worn out and tired before the work week began? How much stronger would her marriage have been if she had more time to spend with my dad? How much better would my relationship have been with my mother had she had the space to be emotionally available to me and our family? The truth is, we will never know because those moments and opportunities have passed.

At the start of my motherhood journey, I found myself emulating many of the things my mother (and other motherly influences around me) were doing because it was a familiar place. I had no other examples, so I trusted what had been demonstrated. Just like my mother, I decided to be a stay-at-home mom with my daughter, Aubrie.

Becoming a mother was one of the proudest moments of my life. At one point, the doctor said that birthing a child would be impossible for me. Aubrie was my miracle baby. I remember breastfeeding her around the clock, dressing her in the cutest dresses and hairbows, teaching her the alphabet and her first words, and singing every Elmo and YouTube nursery song you could think of. It was a blessing to experience my baby saying her first words, eating her first foods, taking her first steps, and making her first friend.

Although on the outside, most people would have thought that I was a picture-perfect mother, the truth was that I was too embarrassed to tell a soul how miserable I was on the inside. I was sleep-deprived, felt isolated, and unfulfilled. I was empty inside. On top of that, I felt guilty talking about it to anyone because in my mind, a "good mom" would suck it up and keep it moving. Further, it was often reinforced in my childhood years that sharing your personal and/or family business with anyone was forbidden. I thought that something was wrong with me to feel the way I felt, and I didn't have the courage to talk about it to anyone. I often wondered in my mind how all the other moms I knew were able to portray motherhood so gracefully.

So, I suffered in silence.

Just as my family's pound cake recipe has been passed down for generations (as mentioned in the introduction), you also have a recipe for your life. It's up to you to decide what parts of the recipe you'll use and what parts of it you'll eliminate. As a mother, it's likely that the decisions, thoughts, and actions you've made at some point in your life were influenced by a mother, father, or guardian figure. For example, you may practice certain traditions, communicate, or discipline your children based on what you've been taught. For many of us, we will either choose to emulate exactly what was done to us or choose to go in a completely different direction. You may even ask yourself why you do certain things only to realize that you've been doing it a certain way because that's what you had been taught to do your entire life.

If you look at your life as a cake recipe, you must learn how to sift through your ingredients (mindsets). You must determine what is healthy for you and what ingredients should be altered. Some of the ingredients may have worked for others but may not be the best for you. *Mama Myths* are unrealistic expectations that society, friends, and family place on moms. They often cause moms to feel pressure to perform (think or act in a particular manner), even when the expectations are completely unrealistic.

When I worked in HR, I would often come across women who were dissatisfied with their work, who were unfulfilled in their life, and who felt as if they were doing just enough to get by because of their obligations as working mothers. The mindset was they had to minimize who they were. They believed it was going to be very difficult to live a full life, make a high income and reach a certain level of success because they were raising a family.

The fact that you're reading this suggests one of two things: you want to change your life, or you feel stuck in a rut. Either way, there's a good chance that you've adopted some mindsets along the way. Some of the mindsets you've adopted are helpful, while others may be keeping you stuck, confused, or dissatisfied with your current situation.

As a new mom, you may have heard all kinds of advice about how to be a "good mom". I can remember the months of my first pregnancy. Everyone, women and even some men who were parents, seemed to carry the "blueprint" for parenting. Everyone had the magic answer and didn't hesitate to give advice on "good parenting."

From one mom I heard, "Burp the baby after every feeding." While another mom would say, "Let the baby burp on their own." One would say, "It's better to breastfeed." Another would say, "It's better to bottle feed." It continued: sleep with the baby vs. let the baby cry it out (or the baby will never let you put them down), Pampers are better than Huggies, organic products vs. products with chemicals, Barney vs. Elmo, Montessori early learning vs. traditional early learning, tomato vs. tomato, and so on.

By the time I gave birth to my baby, I was confused and anxious about living up to the standard that so many around me had set. As a newbie, I couldn't figure it all out. When you think about it, it's absurd to make a mother feel as if there is a one-size fits all approach to motherhood, because every baby is different and so is every mother. Once I began to block out the noise from everyone else's opinion and trust my instincts as a mother, parenthood became easier to manage.

I thought about how this same concept can be applied to anything in life. There will always be people out there with an opinion. People will always have their interpretations about how things should be done. Society will always have an opinion about how people should act, what they should do, and how they should feel. If we allow the opinions of others to dictate how we move in life, we will never be satisfied. Many of the decisions I made and actions I took in a variety of areas of my life were a result of the mindsets created by influences around me. When I began to take more time to discover what was true for me, meaning how did I feel led in my heart to show up as a woman, wife, mom, and boss, I began to rewrite my personal life's script.

We all have Mama Myths that play in our heads, making us doubt ourselves at times. Can you think of any Mama Myths that may be holding you back? For reference, I'm going to share some common ones with you. Some of these may be familiar, but perhaps you haven't talked about them openly. Others may be learned behaviors and thoughts. Take some time to identify the ones that apply to you and see how they're making you think, feel, and show up as a mother.

Mama Myth #1: Moms can't make a high-earning income and raise a family.

Mama Myth #2: The more money moms make and the higher she grows in her business or career, the less time she'll have for her family.

Mama Myth #3: A mother should be dependent on her husband or significant other to provide for the family.

Mama Myth #4: A mother should attend to the household and her children until the children leave the home as adults.

Mama Myth #5: Growing personally and professionally is hard because there isn't enough time to learn anything new while raising a family.

Mama Myth #6: A mother isn't doing her job if she isn't overwhelmed, stressed out, and depressed because those are all part of motherhood.

Mama Myth #7: A mom shouldn't aim for wealth until after retirement.

Mama Myth #8: Everyone else's needs should be met before a mom's needs.

Mama Myth #9: Selfish mothers put themselves first.

Mama Myth #10: A high-achieving, ambitious mom is a selfish mom.

Mama Myth #11: Highly successful career or business moms often have dysfunctional children because they aren't present in the home. Think about what people used to say about the rich and celebrities.

If you're honest with yourself, you've probably already noticed that you've come to believe some of the above myths as true. The reality is that if you believe these are true, you'll likely act on what you believe. Boss Moms think differently. The only way to challenge this way of thinking is to first acknowledge your way of thinking.

Boss Mom Move: Take some time to reflect and write about the Mama Myths that may be playing in your mind when it comes to motherhood and personal success. The following questions will help you understand where your habits come from and how they may limit you. By being aware of what you've adopted, you can assess what patterns you need to start, stop, or continue.

- How have your earlier experiences shaped the mother you are today?
- What habits, thoughts, beliefs, and actions did you develop as a child that may still influence you?
- Are the habits, thoughts, beliefs, and actions you've adopted creating positive or negative outcomes in your life?

- Describe the relationship you have with your children or people the closest to you. Are you cultivating healthy relationships, or do you need work in this area?
- Are you experiencing mom guilt when you make certain decisions?
- Are you doing what you do because that's the way it's always been done, or are you doing it because it aligns with your values and the woman you are today?
- When was the last time you decided to do something based on your values or personal preferences?

By becoming aware of how you're showing up as a mother, you can begin to make small shifts in your thinking that will greatly impact your actions, confidence, and overall fulfillment.

Visit www.bmmdbook.com/resources to download the free version of the Mama Myth exercise.

Chapter 2

The Boss Mom Script

"Whatever we believe about ourselves, and our ability comes true for us."

–Susan L. Taylor

If you ask any mom, they will probably agree that motherhood is hard. It's an understatement to say that becoming a mother isn't what we expected it to be, but it's also not easy for us to admit. So many of us feel alone in that struggle because society has made motherhood so glorified, without acknowledging the realities of being a mom.

I stayed at home with my daughter, Aubrie, for her first year. About 12 months in, I realized that the stay-at-home thing just wasn't for me. I found myself deprived of relationships and activities I had enjoyed over the years.

There were opportunities that I wanted to pursue. There was money that I wanted to make because I didn't want to be solely dependent on my husband to bring in the income for the household. I believed the Mama Myth that I needed to be home with my children for the first couple of years of their life because my mother stayed home with me and my siblings for the first couple of years of our lives. While I commend stay-at-home mothers, it's something that everyone can't do. I knew that to be in a better place for myself, I needed to do something that would fill my cup so that I could serve others outside of my household. I decided to go back into my HR corporate job.

I worked long hours, nights, and weekends when I was in this job. My boss was a micromanager and didn't always give me the flexibility I needed to attend to my child or leave work when I needed to. After contemplating and staying miserable in this role for far too long, I decided to pursue a photography business that I had started earlier during my pregnancy. I finally concluded that if I wanted to live a life with flexibility, have more time for my family, and not have a ceiling on my income potential, entrepreneurship was the way.

I invested a pretty good amount into a coaching program and hired a coach to help me develop a plan to exit from my corporate job into a full-time business. After months of mindset work and facing some harsh realities about myself, I was able to come up with an actionable exit strategy to leave my corporate role and work full-time in my business.

During the pandemic, many people left their jobs to either start businesses or find other opportunities. This mass resignation became known as the Great Resignation across the United States. Well, guess what? That was me in 2017. I had been working diligently to plan for my great resignation.

I remember having visions of handing my resume to my micromanaging boss, sharing the resignation news with my coworkers, celebrating with the ones I loved, possibly shedding a few tears in the process, and giving the deuces to the coworkers who made it a miserable and toxic environment for many of us. I dreamed of the days when I would be home waking up and getting my kids dressed and prepared for school. I would work in my business during the day, pick up my children from school in the early afternoon, and actively converse about their day. I would have enough energy at night to have intimate conversations and moments with my husband. I imagined my Sunday evenings being free from anxiety because I was no longer miserable about going to work on Monday. I envisioned a life of flexibility to travel during the holiday season or throughout the year, participating in classroom parties during the week, and working with people that I enjoyed working with. This action strategy gave me hope, meaning, and a new beginning. My deepest desires - spiritually, mentally, physically, and financially - for me and my family were attached to this plan.

Days and months went by, and I was working on the plan. I made changes personally and professionally. I spent time on getting my finances in order because I knew the only way to obtain this vision would be to have the money to back it up. I joined business networking groups to tap into the world of entrepreneurs and to prepare myself for what was to come.

I don't recall the exact date of my planned resignation, but I do recall it being early fall. As my Great Resignation date approached, I began to doubt the plan. I began to question how I would cover medical benefits for our family. Will we have enough for a decent Christmas for our children if I stop working now? What if I don't have enough clients to cover the bills? What if I decide that photography isn't my thing? Will we be able to maintain our comfortable lifestyle? I found myself second-guessing every part of my plan. Because I had spent all this time and effort working with a coach, I couldn't find the courage to tell anyone about the doubts and fears that plagued me during that period. It was the end of October. My husband and I were in the bedroom.

He looked at me and asked, "Babe, when will you put in your resignation?"

I responded, "I don't think I'm going to."

My husband turned to me in shock.

"All that work you've put into your exit plan, and you've decided not to follow through?" he asked.

"No, babe, I can't do it. I don't think it's the right time. I don't think I'm going to continue with the photography business. I don't think it's the right business for me anymore."

My husband paused for a long moment and looked at me.

He said, "I don't understand why you're making this decision, but I'll support you in whatever you decide. Just know that this job has caused not only you to suffer, but we are all suffering. You haven't been happy in years. I've watched you come home from work, go straight to the tub, and eat dinner in the tub on some evenings. It's been the hardest thing for me to watch. We can't continue this way. What are you going to do?"

I replied, "I don't know, but I don't think this is the right time. I will figure it out. I agree that this can't continue. But I will figure it out."

I felt a whirlwind of emotions during this discussion. I felt embarrassed, disappointed with myself, helpless, and confused.

I couldn't figure out why I had come to that decision, but that's where I landed.

You may ask the same question as my husband. Why would you go through all that planning and investing in a coaching program only to sabotage your plans? Well, sis, it took me years to unlock why I made that decision in 2017. It took years of thought work, therapy, and mindset coaching to find similar patterns and decision-making in other areas of my life. I became more aware of my core beliefs, things I believed to be true or false about myself, many of which were based on past experiences. I found myself examining unmet goals over previous years. I realized that I didn't truly believe I could run a full-time business independently and replace my income. I honestly didn't believe that it was possible for me. My words were saying one thing, but my thoughts and actions were saying something completely different.

The TAD Model

Have you ever found yourself having all the plans in the world? You've had all the tools and support needed to make things happen, but for some reason you just don't follow through. Well sis, if you've found yourself making these same decisions over and over, sabotaging everything you've worked for as I did, I want you to pause for a moment and think about what may have stopped you from achieving some of your goals in the past.

To help unpack why certain goals were not met, I developed the TAD (Thoughts Actions Decisions) model. The TAD model allows you to take a deeper dive into your thoughts, actions, and decisions that may have contributed to an outcome. Here's an example of how I used the TAD Model to better understand my decision not to resign from my HR position.

Assessment of **Thoughts**: I told myself that earning a livable income as an entrepreneur was almost impossible. I was crazy to think that I could go into entrepreneurship when I hadn't seen anyone outside of my husband build a successful business. I didn't have a good relationship with money. I was scared and doubtful, wondering if this plan would work.

Assessment of **Actions**: I used to sign up for business conferences, but I always found excuses not to participate. When I did participate, I failed to make the most of it because I told myself I didn't have time. Most of my time was spent getting ready to quit my job, but I wasn't doing anything to strengthen my belief in my entrepreneurial ideas. I surrounded myself with people who were ok with me staying stuck in the same place. I didn't invest in my future self and would often tell myself I could figure it out on my own.

Assessment of **Decisions**: I decided to not follow through on my exit strategy because I surrendered to my fears rather than my desires. After going through the TAD Assessment, I found that my TADs contradicted everything I wanted, causing me not to follow through on the great resignation plan.

When you find yourself failing to meet some of your goals, take time to reflect on what you could have done differently to reach them.

Where Do You Work?

I come from a family of educators and a few entrepreneurs. The expectation for me was that I would one day be an educator. I was a rebellious child, so I knew those plans would change. I knew early on as a teenager that I wanted to create my own path to success. The way my family and people around me saw entrepreneurship was that entrepreneurs didn't have real jobs and usually struggled to pay the bills.

I can recall when I first started dating my husband. He was one of my first entrepreneurial influences as an adult. He was working in a business partnership with a close friend, and I watched their business go through many highs and lows. Entrepreneurship was something he was passionate about from the beginning.

When my husband and I were dating, my parents asked me 21 questions, like 50 Cent. One of the first ones was, "What does your boyfriend do for work? "My response was, "He's an entrepreneur."

"An entrepreneur? What exactly does that mean? What does he do?" they asked.

"He runs a business selling hair with his friend." I remember the pause in my parents' voices.

"Robyn, does he have a real job?" mom asked.

"It is a real job. He makes money from it," I responded. I could hear the disappointment in my mother's voice.

"Well, if he can take care of you, and as long as he isn't an entrepreneur in the streets, I guess it's ok," my mother said.

I remember immediately having silent anxiety when my mom responded this way. Everything I had been taught about entrepreneurship had me second-guessing my husband's potential at that moment. All I could think of was Tommy in one of my favorite sitcoms, Martin. Tommy would always refer to his "job", but no one ever knew where he worked or what he did. If you're familiar with this show, the running joke every time Tommy mentioned going to work was, "Tommy, you ain't got no job!" It's funny now, but that's all I could think of at the beginning of our relationship because that's the picture that my family had painted. The only way to be successful in marriage and raising a family was by getting your college degree and working a decent-paying job until your children graduated from college. As you can see, these were the mindsets I carried initially when it came to success and business.

You may also find yourself with similar unmet goals and results. You're familiar with success, but in some areas, you struggle to follow through and you're not sure why. Take some time to go through the TAD Assessment. Ask yourself, why am I not following through on what I want? From chapter one, think about the models or examples that have influenced many of your TADs.

Write down the TADs that have led to your outcome. If you find that your TADs aren't representing your desired outcome, it's time to rewrite the scripts that have held you back from achieving your goals.

To complete the TAD exercise, visit www.bmmdbook.com/resources.

Rewrite Your Boss Mom Script

Now that you've taken time to identify the areas of unmet goals and you've assessed your TADs, it's time to rewrite your script. Start with the end in mind. Ask yourself the following questions:

- What would your life look like if you threw all the Mama Myths out and created your own story?
- What would you be pursuing right now? How would your life change?
- What TADs would you demonstrate to make this a reality?
- What would you be doing?
- Who would you be around?
- How would you feel?

Think about those questions. Conversely, think about your moments of achieving certain goals in your life. What were the thoughts, actions, and decisions you notice that led you to accomplish those goals?

Boss Mom Move: Visit www.bmmdbook.com/resources and complete the Boss Mom Script exercise. This guide will help you document your new belief system as a Boss Mom. I would encourage you to read this daily or as often as possible so that the new script will become familiar to you. You'll begin to be more cognizant of how you think, act, and make decisions that affect your life moving forward.

Chapter 3

Rediscover Yourself

"You cannot live to please everyone else. You have to edify, educate, and fulfill your dreams and destiny."

- Viola Davis

Who Are You?

It's no secret that at some point on your motherhood journey, you can lose yourself. Because you're juggling the demands of changing diapers, chauffeuring your children around for extracurricular activities, loading the laundry, cooking meals, responding to work emails, giving your significant other attention, and keeping your career intact, it's easy to lose sight of your interests and passions in the process. Studies show that full-time working and business moms spend 13 hours a day working or at home doing chores. It's easy to get caught up in taking care of everyone else that you don't realize until later how much you've lost yourself.

My husband and I had a recent conversation about how far we've come since our marriage. In May of this year, we will be celebrating 10 years of marriage! We were married for about a year before I got pregnant with Aubrie. I shared with him how looking back, I didn't realize how much I had lost myself in the process of being a first-time mother. When we broke down the timeline, I concluded that for a total of 4 years, my body didn't belong to me. I spent almost one year (and yes, I said one year, because we all know that's how a full-term pregnancy feels) of pregnancy with my daughter. I breastfed for another year.

Shortly after a year of breastfeeding my daughter, we discovered that I was pregnant with my son. My body went through two more years of the same cycle of pregnancy and breastfeeding. If you've given birth to more than one child close in age, you can relate to the hormonal imbalances, changes in your body, and emotional stress you're up against. Raising more than one child under the age of two is certainly not for the faint at heart. On top of that, I was working in a highly stressful job that I mentioned previously. Because I decided to stay in this place of stress for years due to fear, I lost so much of myself in the process.

When my children became more independent, and my husband and I finally adjusted to the new normal, I felt lost and disconnected from myself. I didn't know who I was, and it showed. I didn't know what I wanted, and I had difficulty communicating my needs to my husband. I had to take time to reconnect with myself because things that may have been of interest to me in the past weren't as fulfilling. I knew that the only way to express my wants and needs to the people around me was to rediscover myself in the process.

I also realized that I couldn't set healthy boundaries because I didn't know what those boundaries were. Thankfully, my husband gave me the grace to have more mama moments and discover the essence of myself. Prioritizing your well-being is essential in showing up as a Boss Mom.

Rediscovering yourself can look different to everyone, and like everything else, it's not a one-size-fits-all approach. You must begin dating yourself. Here are some routines you can use to begin the process of self-discovery:

1. **Make time for self-reflection**. Journal or write down a list of your values, interests, goals, or vision. What are the things that are important to you?

2. **Tell your loved ones where you are in the rediscovery process so they can support you**. When I discovered that I had lost myself over the years, it was a difficult conversation to have with my husband. At first, he didn't understand because he hadn't experienced the trauma that my body had been through. I had become a different version of myself from who I was when we first got married, but I wasn't able to pinpoint what exactly had changed. If you find it difficult to express this with your loved ones, I suggest finding a counselor who can help you communicate more effectively.

3. **Examine your self-image**. How do you think and feel about yourself and what is it that you'd like to change? How would you describe yourself to others? How do you feel about your appearance? If you're not wearing clothes that make you feel good or styling your hair in a way that you love, maybe it's time to consider a change. Go and get that bob you've been wanting for years. Take it a step further by adding a hair color that expresses your personality.

4. **Make time to do things you enjoy**. This can include joining that Zumba or Spin Cycling class, reading your favorite

book, putting on a fancy dress and going on a date night, going on a wine tour with your friends, or finding a hobby you can participate in often. You must make a conscious effort to set aside time for activities that give you fulfillment and joy. If you're not sure what brings you joy anymore, reflect on the activities you have enjoyed doing in the past. What activities can you recall that brought you laughter, joy, and excitement?

5. **Seek out new experiences.** One of my favorite topics to discuss with my Wine and Mastermind community is experimentation. During the experimentation process, give yourself a reasonable amount of time to try something new. It's all about testing out what works and what doesn't work. If you've wanted to try out a dance class, go and register for it. If you've always wanted to run that 5k, sign up for the next 5k event in your community. If you want to try something new in the kitchen, go for that recipe you've been dreaming of making. Volunteer at a local organization that may be of interest to you. Set a timeframe to complete the activity and assess whether it's something you'd like to continue.

Write about your experience and what you liked or didn't like about it. The purpose is to get your brain thinking outside of its comfort zone. It's an opportunity to discover new interests and passions. Just like we preach to our children when it comes to trying new food or activities, you'll never know until you try.

6. **Seek counseling from a coach or therapist**. These resources can help you explore and identify your interests. A therapist can help you identify parts of your past that may be

holding you back, and a coach can help you set goals for your future. I believe that having both as part of your support system is essential to self-discovery.

What Does Mama Want?

As I mentioned earlier, I started a business because I wasn't satisfied in my career. Although I went through schooling and earned my bachelor's and master's degrees, the investment that I thought would set me up for success ended up causing financial bondage for our family. Don't get me wrong, I wouldn't trade my college experience for the world. But the thought of having student debt in an amount higher than my take-home pay became unsettling.

At one point, I felt stuck in my career because it was the easiest path to move up the corporate ladder with degrees behind my name. My definition of adulting was to obtain a degree and work in a career that either you love or hate. Either way, you were expected to work until the end if the job paid the bills and provided decent benefits.

I can recall discussing my daddy's career with him years ago. My dad earned his master's degree and started his career as a college professor. Years later, he became a middle school science teacher, which he worked until retirement. I remember asking, "Did you enjoy working in your career throughout all those years?"

He responded, "I enjoyed what I taught, but did I love teaching? No, not all the time. Were there other things that I wanted to pursue? Absolutely. There were many opportunities presented to me throughout my career, but I turned them down. As adults, our jobs aren't to work in things we love; we work to provide a living. And that was my job. Your mom and I wanted to ensure that you all had what you needed and that we could be there to support you, which is why we stayed in the school system. We wanted our summers and holidays off with you all. That's why I want you to consider a teaching job as well. As you grow a family, you'll need the flexibility."

Since this was not the first time my dad (or most of my family members) tried to convince me to become a teacher, I gave a silent eye roll in my head. I made it clear in previous discussions that I didn't want to be a teacher because I knew that I wanted to explore other career options at the time. I also didn't believe I had the same calling as my parents had to become a teacher.

When I think about that talk with my daddy, I realize how much I played this script in my head as I worked in an unfulfilling career throughout the years. I was convinced that as an adult, you must take advantage and work in jobs that are presented to you. You must hope that it works out for you, but it's important that you stay committed to your job.

As I grew in my career, I found myself seeking fulfillment and harmony in my life. For a few years at a time, I'd settle into a job and hope that things would get better, but nothing ever seemed to stick. I was going through the motions, playing the corporate game and faking the funk just to earn a paycheck and support my family's lifestyle.

There was nothing that I found exciting about my job, at all. It became a depressing and lonely career because as an HR leader, you can find yourself isolated from the rest of the organization and you're put on this pedestal as the perfect model of the organization. Because HR is the decision maker and has significant control over how organizations operate, most people stay out of the way of HR leaders. If I had known what I know now, I would have made more of an effort to connect with other HR professionals in similar roles so that I wouldn't have felt as isolated in my career.

Because I had been conditioned to stay in this career after investing so much into it, I had to get real with myself. I didn't know what I wanted. I had just been playing the game of doing what everyone else wanted me to do. I knew that to change, I had to apply some of the same principles I had taught friends and employees who had also experienced similar mindsets. It would take getting crystal clear about what I wanted.

Boss Moms know what they want. Here are ways to brainstorm and discover the things you want in any given season of your life:

1. Break down the areas of your life into 4-6 categories, using a combination of family, relationships, work/career/business, finances, wellness (physical/mental/health and fitness), and spirituality. You can also customize this list based on your own needs.

2. Journal or write out your initial thoughts by answering the following questions:

- What are the things about my {category} that I enjoy doing now?
- What feelings or emotions do I desire to have in my {category}?
- What do I need to change about myself or my current situation to get what I want?
- What thoughts or actions do I need to change?

- What monetary/non-monetary things do I want in my {category}?
- Who are the types of people that I want to be around in my {category}?
- For work, what would my ideal job look like?
- How many hours a week do I want to work and how much money would I ultimately want to make? Note: As Boss Moms, there are no caps.

3. Once you've had time to think about the answers to these questions, begin to assess your why which is included in the next session.

Why Does Mama Want It?

After years of self-discovery and investing in myself personally and professionally, I discovered the concept of "finding your why." Identifying your why is commonly used by leadership gurus and refers to having clarity around your goals, values, and purpose. It's what many identify as the secret sauce to success. Understanding your why can help you make better decisions that align with your values. It can also be a compass in giving you direction and motivation to accomplish your goals.

When you can find greater meaning in what you do daily, you tend to produce better results because you're doing it with love and a sense of meaning. It's a domino effect, as your loved ones, clients, and customers are recipients of the value you provide. Research suggests that for us to carry out some of our biggest goals, there must be some intrinsic motivation attached to the goal. Intrinsic motivation is the source of motivation that comes from within us. The American Psychological Association defines intrinsic motivation as "an incentive to engage in a specific activity that derives from pleasure in the activity itself (e.g., a genuine interest in a subject studied) rather than because of any external benefits that might be obtained (e.g., money, course credits)."

For me, working in a career solely for a paycheck wasn't going to keep me engaged in my work nor sustain my success and happiness in the long term. Making money is an extrinsic reward. The external reward of money is necessary, but my work didn't offer any intrinsic value to my life. Your "why" should reflect long-term goals. Is this something you could see yourself doing 5-10 years from now, and would you be happy doing it?

At the start of my photography business, I remember thinking, If I can just work this full-time, I won't have to worry about working for anyone else. I can move freely and schedule my time how I want to, and make money without a cap. What I realized after a good two years in my business was that my weekends were being sucked up even more with shooting weddings and events. The very thing that I wanted to get away from in my corporate job was the same problem I had created in my business.

I realized that running a wedding photography business wasn't a realistic business plan for the current season in my life. I wanted a better presence in my family's life. I didn't want to be known as a mama machine, who gets everything done around the house, pays the bills, but no one knows much about who she is because she's too consumed with doing everything. I wanted to attend school functions. I wanted to be there when my children came home and needed someone to talk to about their good and bad days. I wanted to make an impact and help more people get through things I struggled with for years. I wanted to help more women to gain the confidence and courage to try new things. I wanted a lucrative income. I wanted a business that didn't require me to be physically present every time I made money. All these reasons added up to my "why," and I could no longer ignore these reasons.

Doing things that are in alignment with what you value is the biggest why you can have in setting your goals and vision for your life. Your desires and values will change as you grow and as things around you change. It's an ongoing assessment. Decide on the things that are working for you now. Whatever things are not working for you, eliminate them from your life until there is a need later. If it doesn't align, set a plan to pivot and change course as needed. Just because you may find that it doesn't align now doesn't mean that will always be the case. It's going to take you being 100% honest with yourself. You must be confident and stand by what you decide because the old scripts and thoughts will show up eventually. You must ask yourself, is your what and why based on what you truly want and who you are, or are they based on the influences of others in your life?

Here are a few questions you can ask yourself to help discover your why:

- Who inspires you and why?
- What activities in your day-to-day bring you excitement and fulfillment?
- What legacy do you want to leave behind?
- What is the impact you would like to make on others?

- Think about your past experiences (positive or negative). What have you learned from these experiences, and how have they shaped your values and goals today?

Boss Mom Move: Take some time to reflect and journal on the questions throughout this chapter.

Chapter 4

Honor Your Whole Self

"Almost everything will work again if you unplug it for a few minutes, including you."

- Anne Lamott

I titled this chapter "Honor Your Whole Self" because it's an honor to take care of yourself. It's an honor to cultivate yourself. It's an honor to allow yourself to rest. When I leaned into that truth, it became easier for me to practice self-care consistently.

It was late summer of 2022, and I was in the process of planning a summit for my business, Wine and Mastermind. As a milestone gift, my husband and children bought me a couple of free weights to elevate my workout game. It was one of the most important gifts I could have received during that time because I'm almost ashamed to tell you how much weight I was lifting. I had outgrown the weights I had been using and it was time for an upgrade. I was anxious to get started with my new set of weights and immediately went to the workout area in our basement to get started. I began doing some exercises because I wanted to get a feel for the new weights. Typically, my weightlifting workouts last 45 minutes to an hour. After about 20 minutes of lifting the heavier set of weights, I began to feel a twinge here and there in parts of my body. At the moment, my pride just wouldn't let me stop. I remember telling myself that it's only been 20 minutes. There's no way I'm getting a good workout in 20 minutes. I continued to power through. Within 25 minutes, I heard my internal voice saying, "Girl, you can't go any further." I remember chuckling to myself and finally stopping.

Oftentimes as moms, we push through things longer than we need to. We power through things because we feel like we must. Your body doesn't lie, sis! In most cases, we place unnecessary obligations on ourselves, adding unnecessary layers of stress.

Unaddressed stress or poor self-care that continues for an extended period can lead to a myriad of issues. Ignoring our well-being can trigger mental and physical health problems, and eventually affect relationships with the people closest to us. When we aren't taking care of ourselves, it often leaves us irritable, detached and functioning on autopilot. It can make being intentional or present with the ones around us challenging. Such behaviors can have a domino effect on our children, causing mental and physical stress in their lives as well.

Throughout my childhood and even through my college years, I played various sports. I've always been an active person and considered myself an all-around athlete. I was a super competitive girl, participating in sports such as softball, track, volleyball, basketball, ping pong, and sometimes football and wrestling with the boys. Yes, I was a true dainty tomgirl. I wanted to look nice, but I was always up for a challenge against the boys. Because I grew up as an athlete, I often rehearsed the script of what a "good athlete" does. I am far from being as athletic as I was back then. However, in that moment of weightlifting, I couldn't help but dream about how I could someday go back to being the fit, heavy-lifting, tough girl. The script I played in my head over 20 years ago was playing out at that moment. A true athlete expected that you would always lift heavy, even when it didn't feel the best because that's when the magic happens. Playing out this script from over 20 years ago wasn't working for my current body setup. Instead of stopping during the first sign of my body telling me to and giving myself the grace to come back the next day, I strained a part of a muscle in my arm because I didn't stop when I should have.

Our bodies give us signals that it's time to pause for a second or to take what I call a "Mama Moment." Sometimes, especially as women, we are so busy taking care of everyone else that we forget to take care of ourselves. While it's important to love and support those we love, too much selflessness can lead to feeling tired, stressed, anxious, having low sex drives, and resentment. It's during these times that I believe it's important for us to pause for a moment and tune in internally.

When I had my son, Evan, I remember going back to work after eight weeks of maternity leave. Between trying to find balance among my spouse, children, myself, my business, and my job, I found myself physically and mentally burned out. My marriage was suffering in the process, and I knew something had to change. The thought of changing my job with two children less than 2 years of age seemed to be further out of reach because daycare and childcare expenses continued to increase. I was still running my photography business on the weekends to bring in additional income. During this time, I remember suffering from physical and mental exhaustion, and I just couldn't keep my head above water. I found myself consistently getting sick, especially from the daycare "coodies" that had been picked up by my children. Despite all the warning signs my body was trying to give me (many of which are listed above), I continued to power through.

One evening, I was working from my home computer and noticed that my vision had become extremely blurry and tunneled. I began to see dark floating spots and quickly closed my computer. As I looked around the room, I noticed that everything in the room began to look similar, and I had gotten very dizzy. I remember my heart racing. It felt as if it was pounding out of my chest. I felt my body getting weaker. It was a Saturday night, and I decided to go to the hospital. At the hospital, they ran several tests on my heart and brain. By the time we left, the doctors couldn't explain why I had been experiencing all of this, which made me worry even more because I knew something wasn't right.

On the following Monday, I went to visit my primary care physician. After her assessment and reviewing the tests from the hospital, my physician looked at me and said, "Mrs. Woods, I think you have anxiety. I think you need to rest." Looking back at her in shock, I took a deep sigh and said, "I know, you're right." She went on to say, "Anxiety is something I see with many of my mothers. You must learn to stop and take time for yourself. Mom, you need to rest." I left my doctor's office with medication to try out and a list of therapists to contact.

My body had been giving me signals well before I had given birth to my son. What I told myself from that visit was that I would never allow myself get to that point again. I committed to taking better care of myself because I never wanted my children to see me in the hospital again if I could help it. I wanted them to see their mother in good health, physically and mentally.

After that experience, I never took self-care lightly again. When I began to put myself first, everything around me started to get better. I began to look, feel, and respond better to my family. I was more present during discussions with the people around me. The more I took care of myself, the more the worst job in the world became significantly better.

In recent years, more working mothers have been diagnosed with anxiety and depression than the general population. A survey by Harris Poll data commissioned by CVS Health found that 42% of working mothers had such a diagnosis, compared to 28% of all Americans. [1]

The survey also showed that working mothers are more likely to experience anxiety and depression than any other group, but they're also the least likely to seek help for their mental health. Four in 10 working mothers don't think their mental health will ever return to its pre-pandemic state. Sis, it's important that you learn to pause and give yourself a Mama Moment. Prioritizing your well-being is the most important thing you can do, not only as a Boss Mom but as a human being. As a Boss Mom, it's essential that you make self-care a necessity and not a luxury.

Take time for yourself to recharge and reconnect with what's most important to you. This can help you be more effective in your relationships because you'll be able to give more of yourself to those around you. It's also an important part of self-care for moms, who often put their own needs on hold so they can tend to the people they love. When you practice self-care, everyone benefits because you're more likely to want to spend quality time with others after taking care of yourself!

I've included a list of self-care principles I've adopted that were critical shifts in my life. Knowing that you are doing your best to cultivate a more holistic approach to your well-being is an important first step to self-care. Self-care is more than just a day of relaxation on your Birthday or Mother's Day. It's about taking time every single day to purposely connect with yourself on a deeper level. Start with one or two new principles and when you start feeling good results (after maybe a few weeks), add another. Don't feel bad if it doesn't work your first or second time. We are all works in progress, and this is a lifestyle change that can take time. The point is to experiment and identify what works for you. One thing to note is that you may be looking for a new and sexy trend here, but the reality is that most of these principles have been around for a while and are backed by science. You hear so many people talking about some of these principles because there's strong evidence to support the benefits.

Self-Care Principles

Set a morning routine. Don't overcomplicate this. The point is to give yourself time to be with yourself and do things that make you feel alive. For me, I enjoy getting up at least thirty minutes to an hour before the household awakes to stretch, exercise, read a book, pray/meditate, or drink a warm cup of lemon water or coffee. I've learned that when I can establish a good start to my day, I'm better able to handle the challenges that may come later. Setting an intention for my morning routine the night before also helps me to avoid decision fatigue or making rushed decisions when I first wake up.

Communicate your needs. As a former HR leader, one of the tools I've learned to be the most effective in meeting your needs is clear communication. I worked with leaders who found themselves spinning their wheels because of gaps between the needs of the leader and the needs of the team. When a leader can get crystal clear about his/her needs, there is a level of respect and collaboration that exists. You can practice the same leadership as the Boss Mom in your home. Communicate what you need for self-care to your family so that you can avoid unnecessary stress and conflict. Learn to set boundaries with people in your life and learn to say no when an ask doesn't fit into your plans.

Here's a sample conversation you can have with your children (or significant other):

> "For the remainder of the afternoon, I'll be taking some time to rest. Do not come in unless it's an emergency or if you cannot get a hold of Dad (your caretaker). In that case, you will need to knock first before entering. When my door is closed, it means I do not want to be disturbed. When the door is open, you are welcome to come in and talk. Resting is important so I can be at my best to care for you better! This is important to me, and I ask that you respect Mama's time."

Communicating and respecting one's needs is a two-way street. Practice what you preach and allow others in your house the grace to have their moments as well.

Make time for rest. Rest is not a reward; it is a necessity. Webster's dictionary defines rest as the freedom from activity or labor, a state of motionlessness or inactivity. The key word here is "inactivity," which means doing nothing! If you find yourself lying down to check emails or taking the day off to clean the home, sis, this is not rest! I've had so many clients and previous team members define rest as getting away from their typical day-to-day only to do more unnecessary busy work. I'd consider that as unplugging, but that is not rest! Start getting in the habit of clearly defining a resting time to do nothing at all. Consider visiting a spa, going to the local coffee shop for a break, unwinding at the beach, or cutting off all electronics to quiet your mind and have a moment to yourself.

Do your best to incorporate good sleep routines for your household. I have struggled in this area since becoming a mother. Depending on your child, you may get lucky enough to have one who always sleeps throughout the night. For me, it's been a rollercoaster since they were babies. We may go for months with both children sleeping throughout the night, but we've come to embrace the unexpected nights of attending to our now 6 and 7-year-old children due to bad dreams, sickness, or just restlessness.

Countless studies show the benefits of sleep, which include increased energy, increased hormonal balance, better mood, immunity boosts, better weight control, and sharper brain function, to name a few. As Boss Moms, we should always strive to get at least seven to eight hours of sleep a night by setting a schedule and sticking to it as best as we can. The reality is that as a mother, the unexpected is expected to happen. Give yourself grace in this area.

Burnout is a serious concern for too many of us, and unfortunately, sleep alone will not eliminate the issue. Research suggests that burnout may be increased by focusing solely on sleep because other key areas of rest have not been addressed. Dr. Saundra Dalton-Smith shares her findings on the seven types of rest that are necessary for optimal health in her book *Sacred Rest*. I've found that most of these areas were lacking in my life before I began my self-care journey. If you'd like to take a deeper dive into the topic of rest, check out my mini-course on Setting Healthier Boundaries so that you can find more rest and eliminate burnout in your day. Visit bmmdbook.com/resources.

Don't overthink a good workout. One of the best things you could do for your mental and physical health outside of resting is to move your body. It's that simple. I used to make this concept harder than it needed to be when I first became a mother. So many of us do. I mentioned earlier that I have an athlete mentality, but I would waste time beating myself up about not having the time to work out for a minimum of 30 minutes. There were times when I just wouldn't work out because I didn't have the right equipment to use. To make my routines less complicated, I began performing basic body warmups and stretches for about 15 minutes daily. I eventually began to incorporate dance into my routine. I would sometimes include my children in the workouts because that was the only time I had to spend with them in the afternoons. I've now established a habit of exercising at least four times weekly for at least 20-30 minutes. If you're just getting started and trying to find time in your day, start with a 5-minute warm-up. Once you find what works for you, commit to a routine that you'll be able to stick with. Don't forget to drink plenty of water and eat nourishing foods that will keep you energized. Many physical problems are caused by a lack of proper nutrition or dehydration.

Find moments of laughter. When was the last time you had a date night or girl's trip? Are you waiting to pamper yourself only on Mother's Day or your birthday, or are you finding moments throughout the year to pause and go out and dance? Make time to laugh! When I need a good belly laugh, I turn on episodes of *Martin* or *The Fresh Prince of Bel Air*. There are several comedy shows on TV that you can also watch. I wasn't gifted in coming up with good jokes, so I intentionally surrounded myself with people who made me laugh. Laughter has been something that's been nourishment to my mental health over the years.

Get out of your head. I hadn't realized it until I began writing this book, but I have been journaling since 2007. Looking back on my thoughts, wins, and losses over the years have reminded me how powerfully my writing journey has served me throughout the years. There is nothing like getting things out of your head and putting them on paper. Journaling was a tool that I've used over the years to improve my emotional health. A growing body of evidence suggests that people who can accept their feelings, rather than trying to suppress them or avoid them altogether, tend to experience better psychological health and positive therapeutic outcomes, including improved moods and reduced anxiety. (Forsyth & Eifert, 2016).

Journaling can help you be mindful, accepting, and aware of your feelings and actions. Writing down your thoughts and feelings can also lower blood pressure, improve lung and liver function, improve psychological well-being, and reduce stress-related visits to the doctor. Taking less than 10-15 minutes a day to write out your thoughts or share moments of gratitude can enhance your well-being in the long run.

Find Inspiration. Read or listen to books, podcasts, or vlogs that inspire and uplift you. I aim to listen to or read something inspirational to feed my spirit for at least 10-15 minutes each day. Find what works best for you.

Don't sleep on the outdoor life. I had never been an outdoor person until I moved to our current neighborhood. We have a trail attached to the neighborhood, and I started walking on it about a year ago. Every time I walk this trail, I come back with the best clarity. I feel lighter, and it feels like I'm lost in nature with my thoughts and God.

Research suggests that staying close to nature has many benefits. People who are close to nature have a lower risk of developing hypertension, cardiac illness, and chronic pain. A strong connection to the natural environment alleviates feelings of social isolation and improves emotional well-being. In addition, it also helps people suffering from mental health issues like attention disorders, mood disorders, and anxiety. Being close to nature can help improve physical problems like hypertension, cardiac illness, and chronic pain.[2]

Consider telework opportunities. Working from home isn't a good fit for everyone. It used to be a far-fetched idea before the pandemic. More people are working from home now than ever before and it's no wonder why so many people who can are seeking this option, especially if they are raising children. According to the U.S. Census, "Households with members who teleworked more frequently reported higher levels of income and education and better health than those in which no one changed their typical in-person work in response to the COVID-

19 pandemic."[3] From personal experience, this was probably one of the most life-changing experiences I've had since I began working. It's been a game-changer in all areas of my life. I have time to see my children after school, and we can talk about their day. I also have time during the day to do household chores, take a walk outside, or simply relax when I need a moment. My mood and quality of life have improved significantly just from making this change in my life.

The downside of telecommuting is that you have to be intentional about staying on track with your work schedule. It's easy to get wrapped up in a task, especially if you're not forced out of your office or home by traffic. The temptation is great to stay glued to your computer screen longer than you need to. However, if you give yourself a hard stop, you'll have more balance and productivity in your day.

Protect your Mental Space. Your mental and physical health goes hand in hand. Listen to your body, but also your mind. If you have consistent thoughts that make you sad, lonely, or depressed, know it is not normal for you to feel that way all the time. When you become a mother, things can change very quickly with your body and mind.

Some people will try to tell you that it will eventually go away, but that may not be the case for everyone, and sis that is ok. You can get back to yourself again. I believe in the power of therapy. Sometimes we mamas need someone to talk to outside of our family and friends, especially if we're playing scripts that aren't serving us. There is nothing wrong with therapy. If I had not had therapy, there is no way I would have gotten to this point. I had days of feeling suicidal as if my life didn't matter and I couldn't contribute to my family. I isolated myself from my family and found myself lacking interest in many things I loved. As I mentioned earlier, journaling was one of the best tools I could have used to clear my mind. Sometimes you just need to write to get everything off your chest. It helps you organize your thoughts and see things differently.

Boss Mom Move: What is one thing that you can commit to doing consistently over the next week or even the next month in terms of your self-care? Tell your friend, your spouse, or your significant other, and keep track of how you feel after a week of activity. If it's something that you enjoy doing and something that you find to be helpful, keep it going.

Visit www.bmmdbook.com/resources to take a deeper dive into setting healthy boundaries and reducing stress and burnout from your life.

Chapter 5

Creating Space

"I'm no longer accepting the things I cannot change. I'm changing the things I cannot accept."

- Angela Davis

I remember a point in my life when I was extremely bitter. I was bitter about the fact that I found myself working 50-60 hours a week, sometimes even more than that. I found myself in a balancing act between family, work, and business. I often felt guilty because my neighbors were able to spend time with their children regularly, while my job required me to work long hours many times during the weekday.

I felt as if I was neglecting everything about my life. My husband, on the other hand, had a laid-back, work-from-home position. He was able to spend more time with the children, but I was limited in my time. In the mornings, I would leave for work before the kids awakened so that I could get to the office before my micromanaging boss arrived. It was the only way for me to keep my sanity and keep my job during this time. By the time I got home from work, I had a few hours before the kids were down for bed. There was just enough time to eat dinner, nurse my son, and read a bedtime story. My weekends typically consisted of doing Aubrie's hair, preparing my hair for the week, which could take up almost a full day depending on the style, running the kids to birthday parties or extracurricular events, editing photos for photography clients, grocery shopping, meal prepping for the following week, going to church, and trying to fit in time with my husband somewhere in between. There was no time for Robyn and no time to form deeper connections with my family.

I knew I wanted to have a bigger presence in my family's life. There was an emptiness inside that you wouldn't have noticed from the outside. I also knew I needed more time for myself after experiencing health issues and being diagnosed with anxiety. I needed time to find another job opportunity and get out of the rut I was in. I had to find a way to fit the things I wanted to do into my schedule. I had grown tired of the Monday blues and was ready to make space for the things that mattered most in my life.

What does it mean to create space? Creating space is about gaining more time in your day to do the things that are important to you. You don't have to be a slave of your own life, despite the examples around you demonstrating that a "good mother" does it all. Sis, let me tell you, that is a lie. If you want to make room for the things you desire to have, more movie nights with your family, better relationships with the people you love, more intimate time with your spouse, a growing business, a higher paying position, or even just a moment to be with yourself, you must create space in your life to obtain those things.

Define your values:

If you want to create more space to do the things that you value, take time to answer the following starter questions:

- What do you value most about your day and week? What are those must-haves?
- Why is this important for you to have more time in your day?
- What would your day look like if you had more time?
- What are the non-negotiable activities you'd be doing frequently?

Once you've taken time to define your core values, find a way to make more space in your day that will protect those values. Here are a few tips I've used along the way to create more space. Keep in mind that some of the options listed below may require an investment, but it's based on your budget and what you find the most beneficial.

Schedule your entire week. Plan your week by separating your duties into categories, such as family, work, business, and finances. I recommend putting the things that are must-haves on the calendar. That way, you can keep your must-haves prioritized and avoid unnecessary conflicts in your schedule, especially when life gets hectic. For example, I try my best not to schedule anything on Friday nights (for our family time), Monday-Thursday between 5 pm-8 pm (for time with my children), one Friday out of the month (for hubby date-nights), and Thursday evenings (for my live video sessions).

Consider Meal prepping. If you don't have time to cook throughout the week, I would suggest food prepping at the beginning of the week or outsourcing food prep services if you're able to make the investment. If you're old school and would rather have 10 pots and pans on the stove simmering, you may find the Instant Pot and Air Fryer to be game changers! These are two great investments I've made for my kitchen over the past couple of years. You will be surprised by the amount of time and energy you save simply by changing the tools you use in the kitchen.

Delegate repetitive tasks. When I first became a mom, as worn out and tired as I was, I felt obligated to do everything possible. Part of that was because my instinct as a mother wouldn't allow me to do less. The other part of me felt that doing everything fulfilled the "good mom" job description. We didn't have family and friends who could help us, and I didn't want to ask on most days.

When I began delegating more, I was able to focus my efforts on tasks that were moving me in the right direction. I learned to trust the people around me, and I became more present with my family. I had the space and time to step away if needed, which made for fewer outbursts of anger toward the people closest to me.

Now that our kids are older, we require that they take care of simple chores before participating in outdoor or extracurricular events during the weekday. They are now responsible for cleaning their dishes, picking up trash around their table area, and cleaning their room daily. It's a win-win because they are learning responsibility, and it takes another job off my list of things to do.

As leaders, we must exercise the same practices we would do at work or in business. It's essential to know when to delegate tasks at home so that you can make your life easier. Knowing when and what to delegate are skills you can practice continually.

Trust that others can handle the job, even when it's not perfect. Oftentimes moms feel that if we don't do it, it's not going to be done right. I hesitated to ask my husband (or frankly, anyone else) to help because I was doubtful that he would give the kids the healthiest sources of food when he was on duty. If you are a control freak like I was during that time, I would suggest communicating exactly what you need. If they don't get it 100% right, learn to accept that you have someone offering to help, and most importantly, your child is healthy overall and getting what he/she needs. Something as simple as hiring a nanny to come in and do household chores for a few hours can make all the difference.

Prepare wardrobes in advance. On Sundays, we have clothes and outfits laid out and ironed for the entire week. You can also hire wash and fold services to assist you with preparing your clothes for the week.

Outsource housecleaning when possible. Every couple of months, we hire cleaners to deep clean the house. You can also hire a cleaning team to come more frequently as needed. On the off months, my husband and I do most of the cleaning in the common areas on weekends.

Dedicate an hour a day to complete your must-haves. The best thing I could have done to accomplish some of the biggest goals over the past few years has been to dedicate at least one hour of my day to knock out tasks that would get me closer to my goals. My coach usually says that an hour a day can change your life. I believe this to be true, especially when you are working in highly demanding jobs, running a business, taking on new projects, or if you have a full-time job and desire to build a business as I did. This rule can be applied to anything you're trying to conquer. When you're not able to set one hour a day due to the unexpected demands of life, give yourself grace and set a backup plan of only 30 minutes a day. This will help you stay focused and avoid overwhelm when multiple tasks are added to your plate.

Dedicate weekly targets. I've joined masterminds in the past to accelerate my progress in reaching business goals. One of the time management methods I learned that worked very well for me was dedicating weekly targets. For example, I would dedicate one week to creating a new sales page and another week to creating a landing page. Once those targets are completed, take time to celebrate the milestone, even if it means doing nothing for the day or drinking a glass of wine. It's the small wins for me. Combining weekly goals and targets with opportunities to check in with accountability partners has helped propel my business in ways I wouldn't have been able to do previously and has been a game changer for me over the past year. Remember to give yourself grace. If you're unable to meet every time commitment every single day, it is fine to pick back up where you left off.

Boss Mom Move: Journal about the values you created at the beginning of this chapter. What values do you want to spend more time cultivating? What kinds of activities would help you live those values more fully? Write out a list of tasks that you could delegate to create more time for the must-haves in your life. Make sure to also list out whom you could assign the task to, if possible. For example, you may decide to assign laundry to your children. You may assign grocery shopping to an online app such as Instacart or curbside pickup. The options are endless. When you've made time for the must-haves, don't forget to add them to your calendar and do your best to stay committed.

Chapter 6

Build your Village

"It takes a village to raise a child, and it takes a tribe to support a mother."

- Robyn Woods

No New Friends?

One thing we can all agree on is that it's hard to make friends as an adult. Many of us are content with the friends we've had over the years. Why make any new ones? I have friends I've known for well over 20 years. I tend to stay in touch with them frequently throughout the year, but because of distance, it's difficult to connect consistently. For the longest time, I operated using the mantra of "no new friends," as one of my favorite artists Drake would say.

A 2021 survey by the American Perspectives Group shows that Americans report fewer close friendships than ever. Respondents claimed to talk and rely less often on their friends for emotional support. The survey also found that working long hours leads to social isolation, and parents who do not get enough adult friend time may experience feelings of loneliness. According to the survey, having too many friends in one area of your life (such as only the workplace) makes you vulnerable to loneliness. The research findings highlight the importance of fostering strong social bonds and being a part of a community.[4]

Immediately after the birth of my second child, the whole idea of "no new friends" was the opposite of what I realized I needed. It was on a weekday. My husband and I had just left the hospital close to downtown Atlanta from my son's appointment. It was almost 5:00 p.m., so we put in the address for my daughter's daycare. The estimated time of arrival showed that we would arrive after 6:30 p.m. due to typical Atlanta rush hour traffic. This is when I started to panic. I was thinking, how will we get to the daycare to pick up Aubrie before it closes? There's no way we will get there before the daycare closes.

I began looking through my phone. I thought to myself, who can pick up my baby that she knows outside of us? She'll panic if she's picked up by a stranger. How will we notify the daycare office if the person isn't already on our emergency contact list? All these thoughts raced through my mind.

Finally, we thought of our former pastor who had lived in the area when we were going through marriage counseling. I decided to make the call, praying that someone would answer, and I was relieved when they did. I spoke with the First Lady of the church, and she immediately rearranged her plans to pick up Aubrie for us. I remember telling the First Lady to make sure she told Aubrie that we were on the way. When we called to speak with Aubrie, I could hear stranger danger in her voice, even at two. But because she listened to our voices, there was some level of calm. Although I was at peace with the fact that Aubrie was in good hands, I couldn't help but worry about how she was feeling about being picked up by someone she barely knew.

This was the reality check that we needed friends and a community. I knew that if we didn't handle this soon, it would only get worse with two children. While my husband was working from home and could do pickup most days, I was determined that we would never be without a backup plan again.

The more I realized how important it was to create community, the more I started putting forth more effort to build relationships. If you find yourself playing the script that you don't need any friends and that you've got things under control, it will be very difficult for you to be a true boss of your own life. The reality is that you can't do it all. You will drop the ball, and you will eventually burn yourself out trying to be superwoman. Take some time to assess your relationships because this is an essential component to building a thriving life as a Boss Mom. Relationships matter. Open yourself up to relationships because we all need them to thrive, whether you're running a business, working in a career, or pursuing a new project that may require other stakeholders.

As I began to open myself up to new relationships, I started by building them with other daycare moms. I would attend school parties and events regularly. One of the best icebreakers I've found to spark conversations with parents is to ask about their children. How old are they? How does your child like school? Is your child napping during the day? Does your child sleep throughout the night? These have been great icebreaker discussions for me in the past. Once you open that first dialogue, the conversation goes from there. Most people will keep the conversation going because what you'll find is that a lot of mothers are seeking those same connections with other mothers. We want to be seen and heard by other moms who get our mama guilt, shame, doubts, insecurities, and even questions about motherhood, because the motherhood journey is not a one-size-fits-all type of thing, right? As I began to build friendships with other moms from the daycare, it was a natural next step for us to introduce our spouses or significant others to one another. Oftentimes, this would happen at birthday or holiday parties. It wasn't the easiest to convince my introverted husband to mix and mingle with strangers he didn't know, but it was part of the investment we were willing to make to build our village.

My husband and I began spending time with other couples to get to know them better. We would go out to lunch or dinner to learn more about each other's values, standards, families, and character. Most of the time, this bond can be established over simple play dates. During the play dates, we took time to assess if we would vibe with the other couple. For example, if we were with a couple who often complained and talked recklessly to each other or their kids, we knew they wouldn't be the best fit for us. We are intentional about not spending time around toxic people because our goal is to thrive, not only as individuals but as parents also. The only way we can thrive in the area of parenthood is by connecting ourselves with other people who desire to thrive in that area as well. The same concept of getting to know the parents will also apply if you are a single parent.

It was the summer of 2020, and we were in the thick of the pandemic. Businesses were closed, people were afraid to interact with others outside of their families, and there was talk about children going back to school virtually. We were planning for Aubrie's first year of kindergarten, as she couldn't finish out her pre-school year due to the pandemic school closures. We decided to move to a neighborhood closer to a school I had been researching for some time. What I quickly noticed was that this neighborhood wasn't like any I had ever been part of. Children of many ages, races, and backgrounds were outside playing. The icing on the cake was that we noticed the parents outside also. After moving into the home and receiving all kinds of welcome gifts and greetings from our new neighbors, it didn't take us long to realize that we were right where we needed to be.

The community I had prayed for and written about in my vision was becoming a reality. What was even more comforting to us was that many of the parents we met had similar values and beliefs. After acquainting ourselves with other parents in the neighborhood and having frequent play dates, we built strong bonds and relationships with one another that I am most grateful for. We now see this as our village. It took work and sacrifice of our time on some days, but it has paid off significantly.

If my children walk up the street, I know they're safe because I know most people on my street by name. I know their families, I know their children, they know us, and I feel comfortable with my children being a part of this village. There have been times when someone ran late to drop off or pick up the children from school, and we helped each other. We have someone we can rely on to support us and pick up the children on our behalf, and we do the same for them. It works both ways. At one point, one neighbor and I decided to alternate weeks to drop our kids off at school. This way, we each had more time in the mornings to get things done. We all need help sometimes, and the best way to get it is to be willing to give it. Don't expect that you'll receive the same help in return because the seeds you sow might come in different seasons but just when you need them.

Superwoman

I can recall several moments during the early stages of my motherhood journey trying to do it all. One time I had some family members visit over the holidays. My son was a little over six months old, and we hosted the family dinner at my home. I wanted my family to feel welcome, and I remember also doing everything I could to make myself look as if I wasn't as tired as I was. When it was time to clean up after the meal, I remember immediately cleaning the kitchen. A family member then asked, "Do you need help?" I immediately replied, "Oh no, I've got it." Within a matter of seconds, my son began to cry for me because he was hungry. I immediately stopped what I was doing and left to nurse my son. When I returned, I noticed that my family had jumped in to clean most of the kitchen. My heart sank in a mix of emotions. On one hand, I felt a sense of relief. On the other hand, I wondered to myself, do they not think I'm able to handle all of this? I eventually settled in a place of contentment and thanked them for helping, but the thought of getting help outside of my husband was a bit unsettling at first. This was something I would often find my mother doing as well.

Have you ever found yourself trying to be superwoman in front of your friends and family? As tired as you are, you would rather do all the cooking, cleaning, and prepping for every event than ask or accept help from others. Maybe you feel it won't be done the way you want it, or it may just be a pride thing like in my case. Telling ourselves that we can do it alone is a recipe for disaster. Sis, you just can't do it all. Start becoming comfortable with giving, asking, and receiving help from others.

Boss Mom Move: Determine over the next week how you can connect with other moms in your community. Write a list of places you can go to find other mothers. For some people, it may not necessarily be in your neighborhood and that's fine. It could be a child's daycare or school event, at your job, in your career industry, birthday parties, membership organizations, and churches, just to name a few. You can also find mom groups virtually. I have found attending conferences to be a great way to connect with other like-minded moms. If you desire to have and become more, you're going to need a village. You need to create a village that is willing to support your goals, and of course, you are willing to support theirs.

Chapter 7

Thriving Despite Setbacks

"You may encounter many defeats, but you must not be defeated. In fact, it may be necessary to encounter the defeats so you can know who you are, what you can rise from, and how you can still come out of it."

— *Maya Angelou*

Have you ever had one of those days where you felt like nothing went right? You wake up exhausted because you stayed up late working on a work project. On top of that, your son had a bad dream, and you and your spouse bump heads early in the morning about who's taking the kids to school because both of you have important meetings. Maybe your team missed a deadline on a project or maybe one of the members of your team calls in sick and you have to step in to do her part. You get an unexpected phone call from the school telling you to pick up your child because she has a fever, and you have an important meeting happening in the afternoon. You've missed breakfast and possibly your coffee time, and you're left frustrated and overwhelmed and it's not even noon yet.

We all have those days when the unexpected happens. You feel raggedy, depleted, and question if you'll make it out of a situation. In most cases, it's not about the complexity of the situation, it's more about how you respond. Having setbacks will never be favorable, but they are necessary to help you cope with changes and grow your mental muscle. Again, your response is key. Do you find yourself quickly reacting to setbacks by raising your voice, speaking disrespectfully to others, losing your temper, or being ready to quit everything you've worked for? Or do you take the lead, stand in the storm and do your best to get through with a positive spirit?

Setbacks and adversity can come in many forms. It could be short-term, like dealing with an injury, losing out on a business deal, or working in a toxic work environment. Or it could be long-term, such as losing a loved one, experiencing job loss, or finding it difficult to grow a business or career. Adversity can be difficult to deal with, but it's important to remember that there is no one right way to handle difficult times. You have to try different approaches until you find what works for you.

This is where resilience comes in. Resilience isn't a fixed trait. It requires keeping the right mindset, perseverance, and flexibility. As a Boss Mom, it's important to stay resilient in the face of change because life will always hand us those days that feel like chaos. You can help your children develop their resilience muscles by building your own. There are several ways to practice resilience. I'll discuss three strategies you can use to practice more resilience as a Boss Mom.

Maintaining Perspective

It was July 2021. We were in the thick of the pandemic. During that time, we had been in our new home for about a year, and we were getting used to the new normal. Everyone was enforcing the use of face masks, and many restaurants only allowed carry-out or drive-thru orders. Our plans for the upcoming July 4th weekend were limited because the Delta Variant was on the rise in our community. The virus was spreading faster than the original COVID-19 strain.

My husband had a procedure on the 1st of July. The night after the surgery, he had come down with a high fever. The next day we learned that he had been diagnosed with COVID. Shortly afterward, my kids and I also tested positive and began having similar symptoms. We were told to quarantine for 10 days, which was the recommendation from the CDC at the time. We were devastated because the July 4th weekend was approaching.

As a mother, I quickly began to shift gears and take care of my family. Although I wasn't feeling the best, my motherly and wifely instincts went into full force. The kids and I were slowly turning the corner, but I noticed that we weren't seeing much improvement in my husband's condition. Since I knew that COVID could get worse before it got better, I was determined to do all I could to help him regain his health.

Unfortunately, my husband's condition had taken a turn for the worse. We rushed him to the hospital, where he was admitted immediately and placed in isolation. The kids and I were left at home unable to visit him because anyone with COVID could not go around hospital patients. The trauma I encountered during this experience felt almost unbearable because all I could think of was the moment when I had unexpectedly lost my father, mother, and brother in 2013. I couldn't wrap my head around losing someone else close to me because I was still grieving my family in many ways.

For the sake of my children and my sanity, I knew I had to find a way to keep my head in the game. I knew that my husband's health was in jeopardy and that many lives were lost to the even more aggressive Delta variant. If my children saw me melt and lose hope, they would likely fall into this same spiral of thoughts as well. Periodically, my children would ask if their dad was going to die. I didn't want to lie to them because I knew it was a 50/50 chance. I would remind them that he was in the best place for treatment and that many people, even hospitalized, had survived this disease. Comforting my children gave me comfort because it brought a sense of normalcy to an otherwise chaotic situation. When you're dealing with things out of your control, it can be tough to stay positive. But when an unexpected situation occurs, try to keep the best possible perspective, even when it looks bad.

Leaning on Your Village

Keeping the right perspective alone wasn't the only thing that pulled me through this unexpected season of my life. I also leaned on my village. This is why I stress the importance of building your village in Chapter 6.

Being on lockdown for 10 days, socially isolating ourselves from others, staying indoors for the most part, and being unable to maintain our normal daily routines, felt like an eternity at times. In chapter 6, I spoke about being open to asking for and accepting help from others. I've always struggled in this area. I was hesitant to tell my neighbors and my distant friends because I didn't want to place an unnecessary burden on them.

After a few days in quarantine, I was contacted by my neighbor, who invited us over because she knew we would be home for the holidays. It was then I had to break the news and inform her that we were all diagnosed with COVID and that Antoine's health wasn't improving. Within 24 hours, we received groceries on our doorstep, cooked meals, phone calls, and texts of encouragement from our community. I was in awe of the support, not only from the neighbor who called but from many of our other neighbors. We had countless people sending prayers, food, money, and words of encouragement. One of the best moments was when we looked outside to see a neighbor cutting the grass in our front and backyard without us asking. I felt extremely grateful to have a village of friends who quickly saw the need and supported our family.

Later in the afternoon, the doctors informed me that my husband's breathing wasn't improving and there was further discussion about him being placed on an oxygen tank. My heart sank. It was starting to get real. I finally called my brothers, family, and friends to make them aware of my husband's condition. I needed prayers. There was one moment when I felt so afraid of losing my husband that all I could do was cry in my closet after my children fell asleep.

The next day, I called one of my church members to share the news. She quickly called another member whom I had been very close with. They prayed with me. They spoke encouraging words, and their words immediately gave me the strength to get myself back up and confront what I had been facing. After the call, I went back downstairs with my children and the energy shifted. We turned on music, danced, sang, and played games for the rest of the day. If I had not reached out to my village, I would have been a wreck, which may have trickled down to my children. Everything shifted when I spoke up and shared what we had been going through. Sometimes, when you're facing a setback, leaning on your support system can make all the difference.

In a less severe situation, such as having challenges on your job or in your business, consider building villages with your coworkers or other business leaders whom you can lean on for support. Sometimes having a village is exactly what you need to get through your most challenging obstacles in life.

Most Things are "Figure-it-out-able"

During my consulting years in HR, I would often remind my business clients and leaders that every problem has a solution. In my opinion, outside of the things beyond our control, most things are "figure-it-out-able." You may not be happy with the result, but as Boss Moms, we are problem solvers. As the saying goes, "there is no one way to skin a cat." Sometimes life throws us a curveball. You're experiencing issues in your relationship with your spouse or best friend, or you forget about your child's project that's due the next morning. You may struggle to find quality clients or hire the right people on your team. Every problem has a solution and it's all about how you approach them.

I always overpack when we go on family vacations. My husband, who always packs the car, often gets frustrated because I insist on bringing along too many things. His pride won't let him ask for help, so I usually give him time to figure out the packing situation. After about 30 minutes, he'll finally ask for my help. I'm always determined to make my luggage fit, whether I have to rearrange it or shove it under or beside seats. In some cases, I have been forced to leave items behind, but in most cases, I can figure it out.

When you have the right perspective, you'll tackle most challenges with the mantra that most things are figure-it-out-able. Take some time to distance yourself from the problem. Sleeping on it and working through it later will usually get you closer to an answer. You can also ask a friend for help when you're stuck. You might be trying to solve a task at work, or maybe you're building a business initiative and can't find the missing piece of the puzzle. It's all about how you look at the problem.

Boss Mom Move: Think about some difficulties you are currently facing. Assess your approach to the situation and write out a plan for finding people in your village who may be able to help you with this problem. Also, brainstorm 3-5 things you can do to solve the problem.

Chapter 8

The Power of Pivots

*"If you don't like something, change it. If you
can't change it, change your attitude."*

-*Maya Angelou*

Is a Pivot Necessary?

Pivoting in life refers to changing direction, such as changing
careers, moving to a new location, or pursuing a new hobby or
interest. The ability to pivot can be a valuable skill, especially
for leaders. As an HR consultant, I helped high performers and
leaders develop throughout their careers, many of which had
already hit their peak. Some people would find themselves
stalled in unfulfilling work roles or with no further opportunities
to advance in their organization. In contrast, others were ready
to move on to other stages of life, such as retirement or career
changes.

Being willing to pivot is a necessary skill because to truly fulfill
our personal and professional needs, there must be alignment.
When you think about alignment, think of things fitting just
right. Imagine a hand fitting perfectly in a glove or a foot fitting
perfectly in a shoe. If something is not a good fit, whether it be

a relationship, a spouse/friend, a career, a business, or even certain customers, you may struggle for a long period to make it work. If it's not a good fit, it's difficult to adjust no matter how hard you try. It may be time for a pivot. The decision to shift in your life depends on your unique life experiences, goals, and values. Deciding to pivot when necessary is a Boss Mom move. Below are a few signs that may indicate the need to pivot in your life:

You feel as if what you are doing no longer aligns with your values. There's a level of resistance or dissatisfaction in what you're doing. I remember being hired for an HR global opportunity. Most of the leadership team were white men over the age of 50. I knew at the beginning of my interview process that the culture would not be the best fit for me, but I took it anyway because they offered a six-figure salary and some flexibility with my schedule. Although I was thankful to have this job and leave the previous job that had almost killed me, it also had its set of challenges.

When the pandemic began, the leadership expectation for me was that I needed to be in the office five days a week because I was part of the leadership team. I was expected to be there from sunup to sundown. No one else on the leadership team cared about my situation of being the only member with small kids at home because most of them had either grown kids, wives, or nannies to help with household duties. Many of the daycares in my area were shutting down due to the pandemic, and I began expressing the need to work from home. The more I began to express the need to take care of my family and set boundaries with my work schedule, the more discrimination, and isolation I experienced from the leadership team.

I wanted to work from home like the rest of our workforce because they clearly showed that working from home was possible and it boosted productivity. I began to see other women in the organization being overlooked for promotions and opportunities because the leadership team felt they didn't have what it took to be a "reliable" leader. However, it had been demonstrated throughout their career. As the discrimination against me and other members of the workforce grew, I knew that it was time to pivot. After financially preparing for months and having discussions with my husband, mentor, and therapist, I decided to resign from the position. This was a pivotal moment for me and my career.

The key here is not to pivot whenever you experience a challenge or if something doesn't work out in the short term. I'm not suggesting that you make emotional decisions. However, there are times when it's necessary to consider both emotional and logical perspectives, which is important and a form of prioritizing your wellness. Be specific about the lifestyle you value most. To me, it did not make sense for me to be in the office five days a week, all hours of the day when my children were home and schools were closed. I ultimately decided to leave the job and explore other opportunities because my body and mind told me it was time to move on. To others, it didn't make sense, but I was at peace with the decision.

About eight months later, I began working for a new organization that a former neighbor referred me to. It is a 100% work-from-home opportunity, and the work schedule better aligns with my values and lifestyle. The management also understands the obstacles and challenges of a working parent, which has helped me succeed more in my professional and personal life. Taking on this opportunity was the best decision I could have made for my career in a long time. Have courage in your choices because this is ultimately about taking care of yourself and creating alignment with the things that matter most to you.

You are no longer happy or fulfilled in your situation. Have you ever been in a relationship with someone who seemed like a good fit at first but turned out to be the opposite? I was guilty of this many times in my early years. As the relationship progressed and more arguments occurred, it became clear that the relationship wasn't going to last because I had lowered my standards just to make things work. After experiencing enough headaches, heartbreaks, disappointments, and unnecessary stress in a relationship, you eventually find the courage to let the relationship go. You may recall making similar mistakes during your early years as well. Perhaps it wasn't in a relationship, but you held on to something way longer than you needed to: a career, relationship, home, car, lifestyle, or mindset. You knew it wasn't the best for you, and you wanted your situation to change. But for some unexplainable reason, you decided to stay there because you were in a place of familiarity or fear. That's likely where some of your resistance may be coming from.

If you find yourself with that inner pulling or urge to move in a different direction, trust yourself and surrender to the tug. We don't trust ourselves enough. Just like you began trusting your mama instincts to take care of your newborn baby, begin trusting yourself to make the right decisions for you. It will sometimes feel uncomfortable because it's not a familiar place, but things will fall into place when you make pivotal decisions in your best interest. You'll begin to tap into opportunities that align with your identity and find more fulfillment in everyday life. Trust the process. Trust yourself.

You are not making progress towards your goals, or you may have lost sight of your goals. This happens to us all at some point in our lives. At the top of the year, most of us set audacious goals. About three months in (or for some of us sooner), life starts living. There is a shift in business, or the unexpected happens. Sometimes you find yourself working years on a project or business only to discover that you aren't making any progress. No matter what you do, nothing sticks. When this happens, it's often a good idea to reevaluate your goals and action steps to determine where a pivot is needed.

You have a new opportunity that's been presented to you. Perhaps this opportunity may be working in a new role or starting a new business venture. I've always wanted to write a book but never thought it was possible since I didn't have "time." I often would tell myself that I would do it later when the kids got older. The opportunity for me to write this book was unexpected. After concluding a business summit I coordinated in October 2022, I had just told a friend that I needed to make space to write my book and stop putting it off. Within a few minutes of saying this, I was contacted with the opportunity to attend a book writing Conference. When I left the Conference, I was inspired to start writing my book. I was given the tools, resources, and support I needed go get it done. I didn't have all the answers, and I wasn't sure how everything would come together, but I had faith. I found a way to pivot and took advantage of an opportunity that may not ever come back around. Sometimes pivoting means taking unexpected risks, especially if they align with your goals and dreams. This decision to pivot and start writing my book has been the best and most life-changing experience for my family and me.

As a Boss Mom, you must choose carefully what you accept into your life. If you're not selective, you could find yourself always feeling displeased, because you haven't taken the time to assess what's true for you. Sometimes, the resistance to pivot in your life may be caused by the recipe (mindsets) you've been handed (as discussed in Chapter 2). You may feel that if you take on a new leadership role it will take away time from your family, or your family might disapprove of you doing so because it may require some travel, and you don't want to appear to be a "bad mom." From those thoughts, you create resistance to making the shift. You start to feel that your wants, needs, and desires should be put on hold for the sake of others.

The Pivot Position

Many don't know this about me, but I used to be a great high school basketball player (at least in my personal opinion). I was a point and shooting guard at my high school for four years. When you're on offense in basketball, you can make a pivot to create space between yourself and the person guarding you. In the pivot position, you have possession of the ball and about five seconds to decide on your next move. To avoid a turnover, you can dribble, pass, or shoot, depending on what's available to you. Use this analogy as a decision to act. As you dribble, you're trying out different strategies, but you don't have all the answers yet. When you pass the ball in life, it means that you have decided to discontinue what you're doing or maybe delegate this task to someone else so it gets done faster. When you shoot the ball, it's a 50/50 chance that it will go through the net. The point is that taking action is risky. You won't know how things will turn out until after you take action.

In either of these scenarios, all are important to do at some point in life. It's up to you to decide which option you'll take when you're in a pivot position. One thing to remember is that if you hold the ball too long in the pivot position, you'll lose it to the other team. In life, if you take too long to decide on something, you may miss out on opportunities that are available during that season of your life.

Boss Moms Move: Now that you've defined your values and determined whether or not a pivot is necessary, here are 5 tips to help you begin your Power Pivot:

1. Write out a list of challenges that you feel may be holding you back.
2. Beside each challenge, identify if you should dribble (take more time to strategize/solve the problem) pass it (delegate or discontinue), or shoot it (take your 50/50 shot) during your pivot process.
3. Commit to making small adjustments along the way. What is one thing you can commit to in the next week, month, or three months to get you where you need to be?
4. Expect it to be uncomfortable and uncertain, but trust that you are moving in alignment with what you want and deserve.
5. Positive self-talk. Remind yourself where you want to be and affirm who you are frequently. Surround yourself with the right people who will support you and speak positively into your life.

Pivoting in life may require significant change. In the process of change, it is normal to feel some level of uncertainty or hesitation as you consider your next transition. In making your next move, make sure to consider counsel from a mentor, advisor, coach, or trusted loved one. However, the ultimate decision should be based on what brings you the most satisfaction and happiness.

Chapter 9

The Boss Mom Map

"We have to decide higher to move beyond our circumstances."

- Marshawn Evans Daniels

In previous chapters, you've taken some time to discover who you are, what you want, and why you want it. In this chapter, we will discuss a simple strategy to help you reach your destination. It's what I call your Boss Mom Map.

At this point in the book, you've uncovered ways that Boss Moms move differently. You've learned how to think differently, take care of your well-being differently, grow relationships differently, and decide differently. You've taken some time to rediscover who you are, and you've gained more clarity about your what and why. Now my friend, it's time to *act* differently. The Boss Mom Map is a blueprint to help you reinvent your life and set goals with small actionable steps.

Why are goals important? [5]According to a Harvard Business Study, 83% of the population does not have goals, 14% have a plan in mind, but goals are unwritten, and only 3% have their goals written down. The 3% who write down their goals are three times more successful than those with unwritten goals. The 14% with unwritten goals are 10 times more likely to succeed than those without any goals at all. This evidence shows how intentional goal setting can set you up for success exponentially.

Here is how the goal-setting process works:

- Define the 4-6 categories you'd like to start working on. Refer to Chapter 3 for category examples.
- Write out at least 1-2 goals/desires you'd like to accomplish for each category within the next three months, six months, and one year.
- Make sure to keep your "why" at the forefront of whatever you decide, because it will serve as your motivator in the long run.

Now it's time to get even more specific. For example, if you wanted to have more flexibility in your day, maybe your goal is to find a work-from-home position and double your income within the next six months to a year.

Next, identify the type of person you'll need to be to accomplish each goal. Start to visualize your future self. How would you think? Whom would you be around? Where would you go? Write those things down.

Lastly, write out the steps you're willing to take to attain the goals that you've set. If you were that person today, how would you act? What routines or habits would you set to align with your goals? Break down your goals into small, actionable steps.

Here are some other tips to consider:

Assess your daily/weekly activities. What would you be doing, and how often would you do it? What opportunities would you seek, and where would you go to find these opportunities?

Create milestones. Where will you set markers and take time to celebrate your accomplishments? Every week? Every two weeks? Monthly?

As I planned for my Wine and Mastermind business summit, I celebrated the small wins weekly to keep my momentum going. If I found a speaker, finished my landing page or social media strategy, I would take time to celebrate, even if that meant me taking time off to unplug.

Visualize your success. Make time to think about your goals and make them visible to you frequently. Visual aids such as vision boards can help keep your goals in front of you. If you meditate, take 5-10 minutes each day to visualize who you are becoming and where you're going. Visualize the people you'll be interacting with, the decisions you'll make, and the confidence you'll have when you step into that room.

Create a backup plan. As mothers, we are all familiar with the unexpected. You may have a child who's experiencing sleep progression, or a child who's sick for days and it throws you off your sleep schedule. Maybe there's a setback in your schedule that you couldn't have predicted. Creating a backup plan helps you stay in motion even when things aren't going as planned.

A few reminders to keep in mind while you're building out your Boss Mom Map:

- Set realistic timelines to complete your goals. If you know you'll need more time to prepare, be honest with yourself and plan accordingly.
- Give yourself grace. That's the reason for the backup plan. But even with the best plans, the unexpected is inevitable. The key is to make progress.
- Keep your wellness a priority. Identify tasks that can be delegated.

Find your Tribe

Seek support and surround yourself with like-minded people who can keep you motivated and on track. Joining a mastermind was one of the best things I could have done in my business. Mastermind groups are composed of like-minded people who frequently meet to hold each other accountable, learn new skills, and share ideas. While running my business and working in my career, I felt like I was in a bubble. I didn't make space to connect with other entrepreneurs because I made the excuse of not having time. When I began to open myself up to other owners and build my community of Boss Moms, not only did I begin to grow personally, but my business grew as well. I began to walk into rooms that were unfamiliar and immerse myself in environments where people were winning. As a previous member of a few masterminds, I highly recommend that you connect with a similar group if you are ready to elevate your success as a Boss Mom.

My organization, Wine and Mastermind, was birthed from my experience and personal success in joining mastermind groups. It's a community of like-minded women ready to take their lives and businesses to the next level. We are motivated, high-achieving women who pour into each other's lives and businesses. You can learn more about this organization by visiting www.wineandmastermind.com.

I would also encourage you to seek guidance from a mentor or coach, as they can help you point out other considerations you may have overlooked. Well-defined goals can take time but having clarity around the steps you'll be taking and how you intend to show up will go a long way with your overall success as a Boss Mom.

Boss Mom Move: Create your full Boss Mom Map by visiting www.bmmdbook.com/resources. Post your Map in a visible place that you can refer to daily. It's important that you keep your goals visible.

Epilogue

Now that you've taken the time to read this book, you're one step closer to prioritizing self-care and valuing rest and rejuvenation. I hope this book will empower you to take better care of yourself and be a stronger leader in your life, personally and professionally. My goal is that you feel more accepted and empowered, with less guilt about the choices you make about your work and life, and simply get more rest.

If you don't care for your well-being, no one else will. The way you honor and prioritize yourself is the way that you are teaching others around you to respect and honor you. When you're able to show up in a way that's true to you and start doing things that are in alignment with what you value, you'll experience healthier relationships, more earning potential, greater impact, and become the best version of yourself and a role model for the ones you love. Taking action and responsibility for your life NOW will leave a generational impact on your family, friends, and the people you are connected to.

This book helped you discover new ways to develop yourself and reach your full potential. By following the principles in this book one small step at a time, you can gradually increase your joy, fulfillment, and financial success if that's what you desire. Here is a recap of some of the key takeaways from the book:

In Chapter 1, we dispelled the myths about motherhood that may have influenced your beliefs and contributed to decisions that prevent you from becoming your best.

In Chapter 2, we discovered the mindsets of your past and how they have served as a guide to what you believe and how you get things done. We rewrote the scripts so you can be present, take action toward your dreams, and achieve what matters most to you.

In Chapter 3, you were provided with steps to get closer to your true self and discover the woman you are today. It's important that you remember these things about yourself so that you do not lose sight of who you are.

In Chapter 4, you learned how to honor your whole self by setting boundaries, delegating, taking time to rejuvenate, and maintaining a healthy mind and body.

In Chapter 5, you were given practical strategies for creating more time to pursue the things that you value and prioritizing self-care.

In Chapter 6, you were given tips on building healthier relationships with other women and finding a tribe of like-minded Boss Moms whom you can support and who can also enhance your life as a mother and boss.

In Chapter 7, we discussed three strategies for overcoming adversity and building your resilience muscle.

In Chapter 8, you learned about the power of making shifts in your life to create alignment with your goals and values.

In Chapter 9, we walked through the blueprint for becoming the woman you were intended to be by taking the necessary steps to have the life you desire.

After reading this book, you will be able to take yourself out on more vacations, staycations, spa days, girl's trips, and exciting new opportunities. Most importantly, you will be able to live with a greater sense of purpose and fulfillment because you have decided to put yourself first.

The best way to begin using what you've learned is to find one chapter you can begin implementing today. Give yourself the grace you need to learn more about yourself throughout this growth journey. Bosses who move differently don't settle for mediocrity. We're ambitious, and we have a strong desire to have more out of life. Sometimes, it comes with making tough decisions. Find the courage to take back your life and be the boss you were created to be. Accept your new beginnings. Accept that you were built differently. Accept that you will become your best self and model that for your children. Make your moves now - because Boss Moms Move Differently.

About the Author

Robyn Woods is a personal development and business strategist for high-achieving professional moms. She is the founder of Wine & Mastermind, a business coaching and mastermind program designed to help entrepreneurial women achieve next-level success. Robyn is committed to creating a community of highly motivated, like-minded women who are working toward building successful companies and families.

Robyn started her career as an HR strategist with multiple Fortune 100 and 500 corporations, where she gained a wealth of experience that now helps her connect boss women to the possibilities of their vision and create frameworks that bring that vision to life.

When she's not working, Robyn enjoys traveling to new places, watching movies, and competing with her husband and two children in board games. She's a singer by heart, and you'll often find her singing around the house, working out, or dancing to Beyonce, Bruno Mars, or 80's or 90's music. She is on a personal journey to help women who struggle to find their voices and fulfill their potential.

Let's stay connected:

Wine and Mastermind Summit 2023:
Visit bmmdbook.com/summit to purchase your tickets for the Wine and Mastermind Summit which will take place on October 13 and 14, 2023.

One-on-one Coaching:

If you want to learn how to work closely with me and reinvent a life that's both professionally and personally fulfilling, let's connect!

Email me at robyn@wineandmastermind.com

Or visit www.bmmdbook.com/coaching

Works Cited

1. https://www.cvshealth.com/news/mental-health/the-mental-health-crisis-of-working-moms.html

2. https://positivepsychology.com/positive-effects-of-nature/

3. https://www.census.gov/library/stories/2021/03/working-from-home-during-the-pandemic.html

4. https://www.scienceofpeople.com/loneliness-statistics/

5. https://thedrivenmama.com/6-steps-how-to-set-goals-that-will-lead-you-to-success-when-starting-something-new/

References

Mom Facts - https://bit.ly/3ZqyEFs

https://www.mother.ly/news/2022-state-of-motherhood-survey/

https://catalystcenterllc.com/why-prioritizing-your-well-being-as-a-parent-is-important/

https://positivepsychology.com/intrinsic-motivation-examples/

The Mental Health Crisis of Working Moms - http://bit.ly/3ZAygEl

https://positivepsychology.com/benefits-of-journaling/

https://positivepsychology.com/positive-effects-of-nature/

The Benefits of Resting and How to Unplug In A Busy World - http://bit.ly/3SKlXmL

Working from Home During the Pandemic - http://bit.ly/41wUd94

The 4D's of Time Management - http://bit.ly/3ZxF59B

Made in the USA
Columbia, SC
29 April 2023